Here's a marvellous set of studies. Elizabeth has served up a rich feast to help us deepen our wonder, gratitude, and trust in the faithfulness and kindness of our loving God. The studies brim with insight, helpful quotes and the kind of questions that not only take us deeper into the Bible but also help us to see God's concern for, and hand in, our whole lives: at home and at work; in church and in the community; from Monday to Saturday, as well as on Sunday.

Mark Greene, Mission Champion, London Institute of Contemporary Christianity

God's faithfulness and his command to us to be faithful were always concepts I took for granted without truly grasping them. *Faithful: Because GOD is* helps us to appropriate these big Bible concepts as truths to live by in everyday life. Elizabeth McQuoid does what the Bible does in this thoroughly God-centred guide: she roots Scripture's command to faithfulness in God's own faithfulness to deliver what he promises for all those trusting in Jesus. Whether you are in the throes of suffering or simply charting a course through our increasingly secularized society, or looking for something for yourself or for your small group, I'd heartily recommend this study guide.

Jonny Ivey, Senior Editor of Heirs Magazine *and co-author of* Silent Cries: Experiencing God's Love after Losing a Baby

GW00458604

Faithful

Because GOD is

Elizabeth McQuoid

BIBLE STUDY RESOURCES FOR
INDIVIDUALS OR SMALL GROUPS

INTER-VARSITY PRESS
36 Causton Street, London SW1P 4ST, England
Email: ivp@ivpbooks.com
Website: www.ivpbooks.com

First published 2021

British Library Cataloguing-in-Publication Data
A catalogue record for this book is available from the British Library.

ISBN: 978–1–78974–339–5
eBook ISBN: 978–1–78974–340–1

Set in Warnock
Typeset in Great Britain by CRB Associates, Potterhanworth, Lincolnshire
Printed in Great Britain by Ashford Colour Press Ltd, Gosport, Hampshire

Produced on paper from sustainable sources.

Inter-Varsity Press publishes Christian books that are true to the Bible and that communicate the gospel, develop discipleship and strengthen the church for its mission in the world.

IVP originated within the Inter-Varsity Fellowship, now the Universities and Colleges Christian Fellowship, a student movement connecting Christian Unions in universities and colleges throughout Great Britain, and a member movement of the International Fellowship of Evangelical Students. Website: www.uccf.org.uk. That historic association is maintained, and all senior IVP staff and committee members subscribe to the UCCF Basis of Faith.

Contents

Introduction

'Where is God? Does he care?'

Through a grainy Zoom screen, tears running down her face, my heartbroken friend asked me those very questions. A close relative had died because of Covid-19, her husband had lost his job and her children were struggling with mental-health issues.

Whether on the scale of world events or personal losses, life confronts us with tough questions, and sorrow narrows our focus on to the here and now. The Bible is realistic about suffering, but it lifts up our heads to see a glorious vision of our God, who loves us zealously and is completely faithful – a covenant-keeping God. He's not faithful on *our* terms, answering our prayers as *we* wish, but he's faithful on *his* terms, utterly trustworthy, even on our darkest day.

God is faithful (Deuteronomy 7:9; 32:4) because he is the true God who always tells the truth. Consequently, he can't help but be faithful to his promises and purposes. What God says, he will do. Daily, we see God's faithfulness in action. He hears us when we pray, forgives us when we repent, purifies us when we 'wash ourselves' with his Word and transforms us into the likeness of Christ.

The supreme example of God's faithfulness is Jesus. Before time began, God put his salvation plan into action to rescue us from sin. He promised a Saviour and, at just the right time, Jesus came into the world, lived here and died in our place. His death paid the penalty for our sin. His resurrection is the firstfruits of the renewal of the cosmos, and the guarantee that we too will be raised to new life and spend eternity with God.

As we wait for God to fulfil the rest of his promises – for Christ to return and establish the new heavens and earth – God calls us, as his image-bearers, to be faithful. We are to show the world what he is like, by being faithful in our single or married state, as workers and gospel witnesses, in the routine of life and in suffering, in church and in our community.

Faithfulness is not just a one-off proclamation of devotion to God but myriad God-honouring decisions taken daily, over many years. It's the decision not to watch a particular TV programme, give in to gossip or miss church. The decision to keep your promise to a colleague, spend time with God in his Word, the Bible, read it with your child, be grateful, forgive others and not take offence easily. Faithfulness is the sum of all these little things and many more. But it is not something we achieve on our own, through gritted teeth. God stands with us, strengthening our resolve and cultivating his Spirit of faithfulness within us (2 Thessalonians 3:3; Galatians 5:22).

The aim of this study guide is not to exhaust the topic but, in a limited way, to showcase God's faithfulness. Its goal is also to extend an invitation to become more and more like the Lord Jesus, to share his character and to grow in his faithfulness.

We can be faithful *because God is*.

SESSION 1

God's faithfulness to himself

▶ GETTING STARTED

Is faithfulness outdated?

In a world of political spin, digital transience and broken relationships, faithfulness may seem like a quaint concept from a bygone era. And yet we value the loyalty of a friend, the commitment of a spouse and the trustworthy word of a business partner. Why? Because we are made in the image of God and he is faithful. This is no minor character trait; God abounds in faithfulness! Above all, he is faithful to himself – to his own character, his word, his purposes and his glory. This allegiance to himself is the root of his relentless faithfulness towards us. Because God is faithful, we have a continual reason to worship him, a sure foundation for our lives, and hope for today and also for eternity.

Read *Exodus 33:18-19; 34:1-2, 4-9*

³³:¹⁸ *Then Moses said, 'Now show me your glory.'*

¹⁹ *And the LORD said, 'I will cause all my goodness to pass in front of you, and I will proclaim my name, the LORD, in your presence . . .* ³⁴:¹ *Chisel out two stone tablets like the first ones, and I will write on them the words that were on the first tablets, which you broke.* ² *Be ready in the morning, and then come up on Mount Sinai . . .'*

⁴ *So Moses chiselled out two stone tablets like the first ones and went up Mount Sinai early in the morning, as the LORD had commanded him; and he carried the two stone tablets in his hands.* ⁵ *Then the LORD came down in the cloud and stood there with him and proclaimed his name, the LORD.* ⁶ *And he passed in front of Moses, proclaiming, 'The LORD, the LORD, the compassionate and gracious God, slow to anger, abounding in love and faithfulness,* ⁷ *maintaining love to thousands, and forgiving wickedness, rebellion and sin. Yet he does not leave the guilty unpunished; he punishes the children and their children for the sin of the parents to the third and fourth generation.'*

⁸ *Moses bowed to the ground at once and worshipped.* ⁹ *'Lord,' he said, 'if I have found favour in your eyes, then let the Lord go with us. Although this is a stiff-necked people, forgive our wickedness and our sin, and take us as your inheritance.'*

FOCUS ON THE THEME

1. Why do we sometimes doubt God's faithfulness?

WHAT DOES THE BIBLE SAY?

God made a covenant with the Israelites: if they obeyed his commands, they would be his 'treasured possession' (Exodus 19:5). But while Moses was on Mount Sinai receiving the Ten Commandments, the people built a golden calf to worship. Incensed at their unfaithfulness, God instructed the people to go into Canaan, the land that he had promised them, but refused to go with them. Here, in Exodus 33:18 – 34:9, Moses asks to know God more intimately and he intercedes on behalf of the people to try to renew the covenant.

2. What was Moses' request and how did God respond? Look at Exodus 33:18–19 and 34:6.

3. What can we learn about God's faithfulness from verse 6?

4. In verse 7, how does God's faithfulness express itself?

5. How did Moses respond to the revelation of God's person and character? See verses 8–9.

◉ **GOING DEEPER**

6. What does God's being faithful to himself actually mean in practice? Look at:
    - Numbers 23:19

    - Isaiah 55:10–11

7. Can our behaviour nullify God's faithfulness? See Romans 3:3–4 and 2 Timothy 2:13.

8. What imagery does Moses use in Deuteronomy 32:4 to convey God's faithfulness? In what ways is this image helpful?

In C. S. Lewis's *The Voyage of the Dawn Treader*, Lucy reads a spell to make hidden things visible. To her surprise, Aslan appears in the doorway:

'Oh, Aslan,' said she, 'it was kind of you to come.'
   'I have been here all the time,' said he, 'but you have just made me visible.'

'Aslan!' said Lucy, almost a little reproachfully. 'Don't make fun of me.
As if anything I could do would make you visible!'
'It did,' said Aslan. 'Do you think I wouldn't obey my own rules?'

(p. 178)

 **LIVING IT OUT**

9. What should our response to God's faithfulness be? Look at:
    • Exodus 34:8–9

    • Lamentations 3:19–24

10. God's faithfulness puts his glory on display.

    (a) Look back – in what ways have you seen God's glory this
         week?

    (b) Look forward – what steps can you take to be more
         intentional about recognizing God's faithfulness this week?

▲ PRAYER TIME

Moses got a glimpse of God's abounding faithfulness and he 'bowed to the ground at once and worshipped' (Exodus 34:8). We have received more than a glimpse. We have our personal experience of God's work in our lives and the testimony of Scripture, as well as Jesus himself as a demonstration of God's relentless faithfulness.

Today, worship God for who he is and the wonderful reality that, because he is faithful to himself, he cannot help but be faithful to us.

⬤ FURTHER STUDY

Exodus 34:6 is echoed on several occasions throughout the Old Testament, for example in Psalm 86:15. Read Psalm 86. What situation is King David facing? Why does he meditate on God's character? How should being sure of God's faithfulness have an impact on our prayer lives?

SESSION 2

God's faithfulness to his promises

▶ GETTING STARTED

Can you remember the last time you broke a promise?

Perhaps you promised to play football with your child, then had to take a work phone call. Maybe you promised your boss you'd have a project completed on time but you just couldn't meet the deadline. Or perhaps you promised your spouse you'd collect groceries on your way home and you simply forgot.

Imagine being able to deliver on every promise – never being overwhelmed by circumstances beyond your control, never forgetting a commitment you'd made or never wilfully choosing to do your own thing instead. God is the only one who has never broken his promises. The Bible is full of his promises to us, and 'no matter how many promises God has made, they are "Yes" in Christ' (2 Corinthians 1:20). Because we know God's character, because we've seen him keep his promises in the past, we can have confidence that all God's promises for the future – Jesus' return, the renewal of creation and our eternal life with him – will be fully realized. We can wait with confidence and hope.

Read *Hebrews 6:13-20*

¹³ *When God made his promise to Abraham, since there was no one greater for him to swear by, he swore by himself,* ¹⁴ *saying, 'I will surely bless you and give you many descendants.'* ¹⁵ *And so after waiting patiently, Abraham received what was promised.*

¹⁶ *People swear by someone greater than themselves, and the oath confirms what is said and puts an end to all argument.* ¹⁷ *Because God wanted to make the unchanging nature of his purpose very clear to the heirs of what was promised, he confirmed it with an oath.* ¹⁸ *God did this so that, by two unchangeable things in which it is impossible for God to lie, we who have fled to take hold of the hope set before us may be greatly encouraged.* ¹⁹ *We have this hope as an anchor for the soul, firm and secure. It enters the inner sanctuary behind the curtain,* ²⁰ *where our forerunner, Jesus, has entered on our behalf. He has become a high priest for ever, in the order of Melchizedek.*

 FOCUS ON THE THEME

1. What happened the last time you broke a promise? How did you feel and what were the results?

 WHAT DOES THE BIBLE SAY?

2. What was God's promise to Abraham (verse 14)?

3. What does God do to emphasize how secure his promise is
    (verses 13 and 16–17)? For whom was this assurance (verse 18)?

4. What is the 'hope' that the writer talks about in verses 18–19?

5. What is the promise for those who have 'fled to hope' (verse 19–20)?

⊙ GOING DEEPER

Let's take a further look at what Hebrews says about God's promises.
Read Hebrews 12:25–29.

6. What has God promised regarding the future?

7. What should our response be to this promise?

8. What promises has God made about life now? Here are a few Bible references to help you to get started.
   - Isaiah 40:29–31

   - Philippians 4:6–7

   - Hebrews 13:5

The Bible is full of God's promises to provide for us spiritually and materially, to never forsake us, to give us peace in times of difficult circumstances, to cause all circumstances to work together for our good, and finally to bring us safely home to glory. Not one of those promises is dependent upon our performance. They are all dependent on the grace of God, given to us through Jesus Christ.

(Jerry Bridges, *Transforming Grace*, p. 72)

 LIVING IT OUT

9. 'And we know that in all things God works for the good of those who love him, who have been called according to his purpose' (Romans 8:28). Why do we sometimes struggle to trust this particular promise of God?

10. What difference does it make to live truly believing in God's promises? Consider how you would respond in the following scenarios:

    • the death of a loved one

    • long-term ill health

    • the betrayal of a spouse or close friend

    • unanswered prayers for fertility

    • the disappointments and stresses of everyday life

    • celebrating achievements and joyous occasions

There is an in-between-ness to this life. God gives us great promises in the gospel. Then He calls us to wait for their fulfilment. He doesn't give us everything right away. He calls us to wait. In between the giving and the fulfilling of God's promises, the waiting can be hard. Sometimes it can seem impossible to endure, because what we're stuck in for now doesn't just fall short of God's great promises. Our experience can be the opposite of God's great promises. Living in-between is not easy. But God's greatest gift is not always what we think. God's greatest gift is Himself. And He does give Himself right now. His own reality and presence and nearness and immediacy and smile: 'The Lord is near to the brokenhearted' (Psalm 34:18), 'The Lord is near to all who call upon Him, to all who call upon Him in truth' (Psalm 145:18). That is not a consolation prize, not something we have to settle for. There is nothing greater in all this world. We don't understand how God draws near and we can't control Him. But this is real, very real, very wonderful. As we stumble forward, God's real presence gives us strength to wait without self-pity but with resilient good cheer.

(Blog post by Ray Ortlund, 'In Between', 26 February 2013)

▲ PRAYER TIME

Meditate on the significance of each of these titles. Jesus is our

- Hope
- Anchor
- Forerunner
- High Priest

Today, worship Christ for who he is and all that he has done for us.

How great you are, Sovereign LORD! There is no one like you, and there is no God but you.

(2 Samuel 7:22)

 # FURTHER STUDY

Take a closer look at how God's promises unfold throughout Scripture.

Look at his covenant promises to Noah (Genesis 9:9–17), Abraham (Genesis 12:1–3; 15:1–21), Moses (Exodus 19:1–6; Deuteronomy 29 – 30), David (2 Samuel 7:1–29) and New Testament believers (Jeremiah 31:31–34; Luke 22:14–20). Consider how these promises were fulfilled and what they mean for us today.

SESSION 3

God's faithfulness to keep me

▶ GETTING STARTED

How can I be sure of eternal life?

Non-Christian friends or family members tell us that we're presumptuous, proud or naive by claiming that we know our eternal destiny. Even without these sceptical voices, few of us are immune to the slivers of doubt that can settle in our souls. Life events throw us off course and our own faithlessness causes us to wonder, 'Can I really be sure that my faith will last until Jesus returns?'

Yes, I can! The good news of the gospel is that our eternal destiny is determined not by our feeble effort but by our triune God. The Father promises to keep to the end those whom he calls to salvation. By his death on the cross, the Son accomplishes that salvation, and the Holy Spirit guarantees that God will finish his sanctifying work within us – that is, making us holy. Because of God's faithfulness, we can be sure that we will be 'blameless' when Jesus returns, ready to share eternity with him.

Read *1 Corinthians 1:1-9*

¹ *Paul, called to be an apostle of Christ Jesus by the will of God, and our brother Sosthenes,*

² *To the church of God in Corinth, to those sanctified in Christ Jesus and called to be his holy people, together with all those everywhere who call on the name of our Lord Jesus Christ – their Lord and ours:*

³ *Grace and peace to you from God our Father and the Lord Jesus Christ.*

⁴ *I always thank my God for you because of his grace given you in Christ Jesus.* ⁵ *For in him you have been enriched in every way – with all kinds of speech and with all knowledge –* ⁶ *God thus confirming our testimony about Christ among you.* ⁷ *Therefore you do not lack any spiritual gift as you eagerly wait for our Lord Jesus Christ to be revealed.* ⁸ *He will also keep you firm to the end, so that you will be blameless on the day of our Lord Jesus Christ.* ⁹ *God is faithful, who has called you into fellowship with his Son, Jesus Christ our Lord.*

 ## FOCUS ON THE THEME

1. Are you sure of your eternal destiny? What causes you to doubt it?

 ## WHAT DOES THE BIBLE SAY?

2. Who 'called' Paul and why (verse 1)?

3. Whom does God call to be his 'people' (verse 2)?

4. Scan the passage.

   (a) What has Jesus done for us in the past (verse 2)?

   (b) What is he doing for us now, in the present (verses 3, 5, 7 and 9)?

   (c) What will he do for us in the future (verses 7–8)?

5. How do we know we will be ready for Christ's return (verses 8–9)?

GOING DEEPER

6. Look at 1 Thessalonians 5:23–24 and Jude 1–2. In which ways do these passages confirm Paul's message in 1 Corinthians 1:1–9 about our eternal security?

7. What argument does Romans 6:1–5 give for guaranteeing that our future is glorious?

If [God] failed somehow to keep his promise to believers to the end and raise them up on the last day he wouldn't just be failing believers; he would be failing Jesus. And that will never happen! [Do] you see? If you are a believer in Christ – united to him by faith – then your salvation is not ultimately grounded in your waffling, wavering commitment to him. It's grounded in God's eternal, unbreakable determination to honor his son by saving you. That's why not one of those the Father has given him will be lost.

(Greg Gilbert, *Assured*, p. 60)

❤ LIVING IT OUT

8. What difference should our being sure of eternal life make to our behaviour now? Look at 1 Corinthians 1:1–9 and Romans 6:1–2 for help in responding.

9.   What would you say to someone who makes these statements?

(a)   'I've wandered too far away from God for too long; I couldn't come back to him now.'

(b)   'My daughter showed signs of faith as a teenager, but is no longer interested in Christian things.'

10.   What means is God using now to keep you trusting him for the long haul?

If you want to get warm, you must stand near the fire: if you want to be wet, you must get into the water. If you want joy, power, peace, eternal life, you must get close to, or even into, the thing that has them. They are not a sort of prize which God could, if He chose, hand out to anyone. They are a great fountain of energy and beauty spurting up at the very centre of reality. If you are close to it, the spray will wet you: if you are not, you will remain dry. Once a man is united to God, how could he not live forever? Once a man is separated from God, what can he do but wither and die?

(C. S. Lewis, *Mere Christianity*, pp. 176–177)

▲ PRAYER TIME

Today, praise God for his sustaining power. With King David, we say, 'Who am I, Lord God, and what is my family, that you have brought me this far?' (1 Chronicles 17:16).

Pray for members of your group, young people in your church and new Christians you know to persevere in the faith, to be sure of their eternal destiny, while 'eagerly' waiting (1 Corinthians 1:7) for Jesus' return.

Pray for God to draw back to himself those whom you love who have wandered away from him.

To him who is able to keep you from stumbling and to present you before his glorious presence without fault and with great joy – to the only God our Saviour be glory, majesty, power and authority, through Jesus Christ our Lord, before all ages, now and for evermore! Amen.

(Jude 24–25)

● FURTHER STUDY

Romans 8:29–30 is often called the 'golden chain' because it reveals the continuing and unbreakable work that God is doing in our lives – from before we knew him until we are made like him.

Study these verses: look up the verbs in a concordance and reflect on the promises, comfort and challenge given. The following books may also be helpful:

Joel Beeke, *Knowing and Growing in Assurance of Faith* (Christian Focus, 2017)

Greg Gilbert, *Assured: Discover Grace, Let Go of Guilt, and Rest in Your Salvation* (Baker, 2019)

SESSION 4

God's faithfulness to forgive me

▶ GETTING STARTED

'I [*name a sin*] again!'

Fill in the blank:

> 'I lost my temper again!'
> 'I gave in and looked at pornography again!'
> 'I made my own plans before I asked God for help again!'

We are aware of our propensity to sin, and sometimes we wonder whether we have exhausted God's patience: 'How can he possibly stick with me when I keep on failing him?'

The Bible is staggering in its response. God demonstrates his faithfulness to his wayward people by sending Jesus to pay for our unfaithfulness. At Calvary, Jesus willingly took my place, absorbed the penalty for my sin and now promises, 'If we confess our sins, he is faithful and just and will forgive us our sins and purify us from all unrighteousness' (1 John 1:9). There is no duty that I have to perform, no special incantation I have to recite, no hoop to jump through. I simply come to Christ in repentance. The cross stands as a testament not only to the horror of sin but also to God's desire to deal with it. He doesn't dole out forgiveness meagrely or incrementally, but eagerly and lavishly. Is the real problem, perhaps, not God's willingness to forgive but our willingness to believe it?

Read *Psalm 32*

¹ *Blessed is the one*
   whose transgressions are forgiven,
   whose sins are covered.
²*Blessed is the one*
   whose sin the LORD does not count against them
   and in whose spirit is no deceit.

³*When I kept silent,*
   my bones wasted away
   through my groaning all day long.
⁴*For day and night*
   your hand was heavy on me;
my strength was sapped
   as in the heat of summer.

⁵*Then I acknowledged my sin to you*
   and did not cover up my iniquity.
I said, 'I will confess
   my transgressions to the LORD.'
And you forgave
   the guilt of my sin.

⁶*Therefore let all the faithful pray to you*
   while you may be found;
surely the rising of the mighty waters
   will not reach them.
⁷*You are my hiding-place;*
   you will protect me from trouble
   and surround me with songs of deliverance.

⁸*I will instruct you and teach you in the way you should go;*
   I will counsel you with my loving eye on you.
⁹*Do not be like the horse or the mule,*
   which have no understanding
but must be controlled by bit and bridle
   or they will not come to you.

> [10] *Many are the woes of the wicked,*
>   *but the LORD's unfailing love*
>   *surrounds the one who trusts in him.*
>
> [11] *Rejoice in the LORD and be glad, you righteous;*
>   *sing, all you who are upright in heart!*

FOCUS ON THE THEME

1. Why do we struggle to accept God's forgiveness?

WHAT DOES THE BIBLE SAY?

2. How does David feel:
    *   before he has been forgiven (verses 3–4)?

    *   after he has been forgiven (verses 1–2)?

3. What did David have to do to receive forgiveness (verse 5)?

4. What was God's response to David's actions in verse 5?

5. Having been forgiven, what were David's new priorities
    (verses 6–11)?

Wherever Jesus sees faith, he has forgiveness on a hair trigger.

(Glen Scrivener, *321*, p. 19)

⊙ GOING DEEPER

6. How can we be sure that God will keep on forgiving us? Look at
    1 John 2:1–2.

7. How does God feel about forgiving us? See:
    *   Psalm 103:1–4

    *   John 3:16

- Ephesians 1:7–8

God [is] eager to put away sins. Because the sacrifice of His Son is of such infinite value, He delights to apply it to sinful men and women. God is not a reluctant forgiver; He is a joyous one. His justice having been satisfied and His wrath having been exhausted, He is now eager to extend His forgiveness to all who trust in His Son as their propitiatory sacrifice. He hurls our sins overboard (Micah 7:19). Corrie ten Boom, a dear saint of the last century, used to say, 'And then he puts up a sign saying, "No fishing allowed."' Why would she say that? Because she knew that we tend to drag up our old sins, that we tend to live under a vague sense of guilt. She knew that we are not nearly as vigorous in appropriating God's forgiveness as He is in extending it. Consequently, instead of living in the sunshine of God's forgiveness through Christ, we tend to live under an overcast sky of guilt most of the time.

(Jerry Bridges, *The Gospel for Real Life*, p. 67)

8. Reflect again on Psalm 32. What do you value most about God's forgiveness?

♥ LIVING IT OUT

9. What do you do when you become aware of sin in your life?
   To what extent are you like King David when it comes to dealing with sin and accepting God's forgiveness?

10. While we might accept God's forgiveness, sometimes guilt still lingers. What steps can we take to get rid of guilt and enjoy the forgiveness that Christ has won for us?

You don't have to drag into the new day the paralyzing burden of yesterday's sin, weakness, foolishness, and failure. You don't have to fear what will be exposed next. You don't have work to portray to yourself and others a person you're not. You can be genuine and honest about places where you need to grow. You've been blessed with forgiveness that allows the next day to be a new day, free from the guilt of yesterday. His forgiveness allows you to own your sin, learn your lessons, and move forward with faith and joy.

(Paul Tripp, 'Each Morning in Ministry', 9 September 2012)

 PRAYER TIME

Use the acronym ACTS to aid your prayers.

Adoration	worship God for his faithful love and forgiveness, clearly demonstrated at Calvary
Confession	in silence, confess your own sin before God
Thanksgiving	thank Jesus for dying in your place, paying the penalty for sin, and making forgiveness possible
Supplication	ask God to help you to forgive individuals who have hurt you, and to share the gospel message with those who have never heard about his forgiveness

 FURTHER STUDY

David's adultery with Bathsheba and subsequent murder of her husband Uriah was possibly the context for Psalm 32 and certainly for Psalm 51. What does Psalm 51 teach us about the need, means and results of forgiveness?

SESSION 5

Our faithfulness to God in the daily routine

▶ GETTING STARTED

Would your friends describe you as 'faithful'?

A man wanted to show his devotion to God. Very pleased with himself, he presented God with a cheque for £100,000. God returned it to him, saying, 'Give it to me 50p, £1, £5 at a time, day after day, for the rest of your life.'

In a sense, one-off, extravagant displays are easy. It is far harder to prove your devotion in small, unremarkable, mundane acts. Yet this is what God calls most of us to – to be faithful to God in our daily decisions, words and thoughts; to be faithful with our money and time, in our relationships and at work, with a painstaking perseverance that is rarely applauded. Jesus' words, 'Well done, good and faithful servant!' (Matthew 25:21), are reserved for those who press on in this ordinary obedience. This everyday faithfulness over the long haul is hardly noticeable at the time, it's sometimes inspirational with hindsight, but it's always precious to God.

Read *Ruth 2:1-12*

¹ *Now Naomi had a relative on her husband's side, a man of standing from the clan of Elimelek, whose name was Boaz.*

²*And Ruth the Moabite said to Naomi, 'Let me go to the fields and pick up the leftover grain behind anyone in whose eyes I find favour.'*

Naomi said to her, 'Go ahead, my daughter.' ³*So she went out, entered a field and began to glean behind the harvesters. As it turned out, she was working in a field belonging to Boaz, who was from the clan of Elimelek.*

⁴*Just then Boaz arrived from Bethlehem and greeted the harvesters, 'The LORD be with you!'*

'The LORD bless you!' they answered.

⁵*Boaz asked the overseer of his harvesters, 'Who does that young woman belong to?'*

⁶*The overseer replied, 'She is the Moabite who came back from Moab with Naomi.* ⁷*She said, 'Please let me glean and gather among the sheaves behind the harvesters.' She came into the field and has remained here from morning till now, except for a short rest in the shelter.'*

⁸*So Boaz said to Ruth, 'My daughter, listen to me. Don't go and glean in another field and don't go away from here. Stay here with the women who work for me.* ⁹*Watch the field where the men are harvesting, and follow along after the women. I have told the men not to lay a hand on you. And whenever you are thirsty, go and get a drink from the water jars the men have filled.'*

¹⁰*At this, she bowed down with her face to the ground. She asked him, 'Why have I found such favour in your eyes that you notice me – a foreigner?'*

¹¹*Boaz replied, 'I've been told all about what you have done for your mother-in-law since the death of your husband – how you left your father and mother and your homeland and came to live with a people you did not know before.* ¹²*May the LORD repay you for what you have done. May you be richly rewarded by the LORD, the God of Israel, under whose wings you have come to take refuge.'*

FOCUS ON THE THEME

1. Think about the 'faithful' Christians that you know. What characteristics mark them out as faithful? Which habits have they cultivated?

WHAT DOES THE BIBLE SAY?

Naomi, her husband and two sons had left the famine in Bethlehem to settle in Moab. The boys married Moabite women, but disaster soon struck. Naomi's husband and sons died, leaving three widows. We pick up the story in Ruth 2. With the famine over, Naomi returned to Bethlehem. Her daughter-in-law Ruth had insisted on returning with her so that they could face their desperate situation together.

2. How does Ruth demonstrate faithfulness:
    *   to her mother-in-law (verses 6 and 11)?

    *   in her work (verses 2 and 7)?

3. Look at Ruth 1:16–17. What was the reason for Ruth's faithfulness?

4. What was Boaz's reaction to Ruth's endeavours (verses 8–12)?

5. How did God use Ruth's faithfulness to provide for her and Naomi (verses 1–3 and 8)?

◎ GOING DEEPER

6. According to Psalm 15, what does faithfulness to God look like in daily life?

Common, everyday choices are the guts of discipleship.

(Michael Kelley, *Boring*, p. 66)

7. What does faithfulness to God mean for our commitment to the people in our church? The following verses provide a few examples:
   • 1 Peter 4:9–11

- Colossians 3:12–17

- 2 Corinthians 9:7

8. What are the marks of a faithful friend? Look at 1 Samuel 18:1–4; 19:4; 23:15–17 for some ideas.

♥ LIVING IT OUT

9. Think through the routine of your life – the relationships and responsibilities that you have. What would it look like to be more faithful in these areas?

10. Consider what we have learnt about God from the Bible verses that we have studied in this session. What encouragement does God give us to keep being faithful in the ordinary routines of life?

Many of us long to follow Jesus more closely, but we are more focused on our present circumstances than on a long view of faithfulness ... But a lifetime marked by steadfast faith doesn't happen overnight. It's built upon years and months of many ordinary days of ordinary perseverance. Though beautiful when traced in decades of retrospect, faithfulness is unremarkable in real-time practice.

(Glenna Marshall, *Everyday Faithfulness*, p. 19)

PRAYER TIME

Pray through the routine of your day:

- for the people you talk to
- about the decisions you face
- about the tasks you complete

Ask God for his help to be faithful – to take the action, to show the love, to apply the effort, to do what is required – today. Pray the same prayer tomorrow and every day.

Small, ordinary decisions made every day to love Jesus more, to look at him more, to cling a little tighter to him today than we did yesterday—these are the ordinary steps down the path of lifelong faithfulness.

(Glenna Marshall, *Everyday Faithfulness*, p. 148)

FURTHER STUDY

If you'd like to think more about how to be faithful to God in the daily routines of life, the following books may be helpful:

Michael Kelley, *Boring: Finding an Extraordinary God in an Ordinary Life* (Broadman & Holman, 2013)

Glenna Marshall, *Everyday Faithfulness: The Beauty of Ordinary Perseverance in a Demanding World* (Crossway, 2020)

For church leaders and those involved in ministry, Paul Mallard's *Staying Fresh: Serving with Joy* (IVP, 2015) gives practical insights and encouragement to stay faithful for the long haul.

SESSION 6

Our faithfulness to God in hard times

▶ GETTING STARTED

'Where is God? Does he care? Why me? Why now?'

Remember the friend I mentioned in the Introduction? Hard times bring with them a barrage of questions. Suffering catches us off guard, perhaps because we have believed the lie that if we look after our health, pursue the right career and seek fulfilling relationships, then we'll avoid grief. But . . . we can't. Suffering is inevitable. God could put an end to our difficulties but, usually, he chooses not to because he knows something that we are reluctant to accept – suffering has value. He doesn't delight in our pain or minimize our agony; he allows it because it achieves in us something little else can – a dependence on him and a longing for future glory. The value, of course, isn't directly proportionate to the suffering itself but, rather, our willingness to lean closer in to God. Each new experience of suffering is an opportunity to exercise faithfulness – to keep trusting and loving, and to walk more closely with our heavenly Father.

Read *Hebrews 12:1-11*

¹*Therefore, since we are surrounded by such a great cloud of witnesses, let us throw off everything that hinders and the sin that so easily entangles. And let us run with perseverance the race marked out for us,* ²*fixing our eyes on Jesus, the pioneer and perfecter of faith. For the joy that was set before him he endured the cross, scorning its shame, and sat down at the right hand of the throne of God.* ³*Consider him who endured such opposition from sinners, so that you will not grow weary and lose heart.*

⁴*In your struggle against sin, you have not yet resisted to the point of shedding your blood.* ⁵*And have you completely forgotten this word of encouragement that addresses you as a father addresses his son? It says,*

> '*My son, do not make light of the Lord's discipline,*
> *and do not lose heart when he rebukes you,*
> ⁶*because the Lord disciplines the one he loves,*
> *and he chastens everyone he accepts as his son.*'

⁷*Endure hardship as discipline; God is treating you as his children. For what children are not disciplined by their father?* ⁸*If you are not disciplined – and everyone undergoes discipline – then you are not legitimate, not true sons and daughters at all.* ⁹*Moreover, we have all had human fathers who disciplined us and we respected them for it. How much more should we submit to the Father of spirits and live!* ¹⁰*They disciplined us for a little while as they thought best; but God disciplines us for our good, in order that we may share in his holiness.* ¹¹*No discipline seems pleasant at the time, but painful. Later on, however, it produces a harvest of righteousness and peace for those who have been trained by it.*

 FOCUS ON THE THEME

1. Think about a hardship you have suffered in the past. Did the experience make you feel closer to God or not? Explain your answer.

WHAT DOES THE BIBLE SAY?

2. Why does verse 2 encourage us to fix 'our eyes on Jesus'?

3. What 'word of encouragement' do we need to remember during hard times (verses 5–8)?

4. How should we respond to suffering (verses 5–9)?

5. What is the result of suffering (verses 10–11)?

The question we must always ask of suffering is this: What could possibly be worth it? Jesus's flabbergasting claim is that he is . . . Suffering is not an embarrassment to the Christian faith. It is the thread with which Christ's name is stitched into our lives.

(Rebecca McLaughlin, *Confronting Christianity*, pp. 200 and 205)

⊙ GOING DEEPER

6. Suffering caused the psalmist's faith to waver, but what did he do to revive it? Look at Psalm 77:7–15.

7. How does knowing what God is achieving through your suffering help you to remain faithful? Look at:
    - 2 Corinthians 12:7b–10

    - James 1:2–4

8. What does God promise to those dealing with difficulties? See:
    - Isaiah 43:1–2

- 2 Corinthians 4:16–17

Christianity teaches that, contra fatalism, suffering is overwhelming; contra Buddhism, suffering is real; contra karma, suffering is often unfair; but contra secularism, suffering is meaningful. There is a purpose to it, and if faced rightly, it can drive us like a nail deep into the love of God and into more stability and spiritual power than you can imagine.

(Timothy Keller, *Walking with God through Pain and Suffering*, p. 30)

 LIVING IT OUT

9. Remembering God's faithfulness in the past often helps us to endure and press on. The prophet Samuel told the Israelites, 'But be sure to fear the Lord and serve him faithfully with all your heart; consider what great things he has done for you' (1 Samuel 12:24).

   (a) Share with the group a specific example of God's faithfulness to you in the past.

   (b) In what ways does this example encourage your present faithfulness?

10. What do you think God wants to achieve through this time of hardship in your life? Is there a lesson he wants you to learn, a truth he wants you to believe or a promise he wants you to cling to?

▲ PRAYER TIME

Today, as you pray about your own suffering and grief, asking God to help you remain faithful, cling to his faithfulness. Turn to God for strength, comfort and hope. Find in him a refuge for your soul.

He will cover you with his feathers,
and under his wings you will find refuge;
his faithfulness will be your shield and rampart.
(Psalm 91:4)

● FURTHER STUDY

There have been many books written to help us to stay faithful in the midst of suffering. You may find the following titles helpful:

D. A. Carson, *How Long, O Lord? Reflections on Suffering and Evil* (IVP, 1990)

Sharon Hastings, *Wrestling with My Thoughts: A Doctor with Severe Mental Illness Discovers Strength* (IVP, 2020)

Timothy Keller, *Walking with God through Pain and Suffering* (Hodder & Stoughton, 2013)

Paul Mallard, *Invest Your Suffering: Unexpected Intimacy with a Loving God* (IVP, 2013)

Paul David Tripp, *Suffering: Gospel Hope When Life Doesn't Make Sense* (Crossway, 2018)

Kristen Wetherall and Sarah Walton, *Hope When It Hurts: Biblical Reflections to Help You Grasp God's Purpose in Your Suffering* (The Good Book Company, 2017)

Our faithfulness to God as citizens in society

▶ GETTING STARTED

What does faithfulness look like in today's world?

In the West, the Christian world view is clashing increasingly with contemporary values. Many young people grow up knowing nothing of the gospel message.

So, what does that mean for how we interact with people in our workplaces and communities? Rather than cling on to the assumption that there should be acceptance – or even primacy – given to our beliefs, perhaps it is better to start seeing ourselves as the early believers did – that is, as exiles, foreigners on our way home. We may feel dislocated and, at times, uncertain but our change of status is not all bad. Being an exile trims the fat off flabby faith and reorientates us towards rigorous discipleship. It forces us to ask hard questions about how to live well as witnesses and worshippers in society. It sharpens our focus on Christ and what really matters – now and for eternity.

Read *Daniel 1:1-21*

¹ *In the third year of the reign of Jehoiakim king of Judah, Nebuchadnezzar king of Babylon came to Jerusalem and besieged it.* ² *And the Lord delivered Jehoiakim king of Judah into his hand, along with some of the articles from the temple of God. These he carried off to the temple of his god in Babylonia and put in the treasure-house of his god.*

³ *Then the king ordered Ashpenaz, chief of his court officials, to bring into the king's service some of the Israelites from the royal family and the nobility –* ⁴ *young men without any physical defect, handsome, showing aptitude for every kind of learning, well informed, quick to understand, and qualified to serve in the king's palace. He was to teach them the language and literature of the Babylonians.* ⁵ *The king assigned them a daily amount of food and wine from the king's table. They were to be trained for three years, and after that they were to enter the king's service.*

⁶ *Among those who were chosen were some from Judah: Daniel, Hananiah, Mishael and Azariah.* ⁷ *The chief official gave them new names: to Daniel, the name Belteshazzar; to Hananiah, Shadrach; to Mishael, Meshach; and to Azariah, Abednego.*

⁸ *But Daniel resolved not to defile himself with the royal food and wine, and he asked the chief official for permission not to defile himself in this way.* ⁹ *Now God had caused the official to show favour and compassion to Daniel,* ¹⁰ *but the official told Daniel, 'I am afraid of my lord the king, who has assigned your food and drink. Why should he see you looking worse than the other young men of your age? The king would then have my head because of you.'*

¹¹ *Daniel then said to the guard whom the chief official had appointed over Daniel, Hananiah, Mishael and Azariah,* ¹² *'Please test your servants for ten days: give us nothing but vegetables to eat and water to drink.* ¹³ *Then compare our appearance with that of the young men who eat the royal food, and treat your servants in accordance with what you see.'* ¹⁴ *So he agreed to this and tested them for ten days.*

¹⁵ *At the end of the ten days they looked healthier and better nourished than any of the young men who ate the royal food.* ¹⁶ *So the guard took away their choice food and the wine they were to drink and gave them vegetables instead.*

> ^{17}*To these four young men God gave knowledge and understanding of all kinds of literature and learning. And Daniel could understand visions and dreams of all kinds.*
>
> ^{18}*At the end of the time set by the king to bring them into his service, the chief official presented them to Nebuchadnezzar.* ^{19}*The king talked with them, and he found none equal to Daniel, Hananiah, Mishael and Azariah; so they entered the king's service.* ^{20}*In every matter of wisdom and understanding about which the king questioned them, he found them ten times better than all the magicians and enchanters in his whole kingdom.*
>
> ^{21}*And Daniel remained there until the first year of King Cyrus.*

FOCUS ON THE THEME

1.   What do you find most difficult about being a Christian in today's society?

WHAT DOES THE BIBLE SAY?

2.   Describe what had happened to Daniel and his friends (verses 1–6).

3.   What compromises did Daniel make while living in exile? Where did he draw the line (verses 3–8)?

4. How would you describe the *way* in which Daniel took his stand? What was his attitude to authority (verses 8–16)?

5. How did God help Daniel to remain faithful in the king's court (verses 9 and 17)?

◉ GOING DEEPER

6. Scan Daniel 6:1–14. Daniel is still living in exile and his faithfulness to God is about to be tested again.

    (a) What was the only way in which Daniel could be undermined by his contemporaries?

    (b) Which spiritual discipline kept Daniel faithful to God in Babylon?

    (c) What were Daniel's non-negotiable principles?

Kevin DeYoung offers a number of helpful insights on faithfulness in his books, for example:

We don't get to pick the age we will live in, and we don't get to choose all the struggles we will face. Faithfulness is ours to choose; the shape of faithfulness is God's to determine.

(Kevin DeYoung, *What Does the Bible Really Teach about Homosexuality?*)

7.   Look at Jeremiah 29:4–7. What do we learn about how to live as exiles?

8.   Daniel's *public* faithfulness to God in Babylon was possible only because he'd nurtured his *personal* walk with God, cultivating spiritual disciplines. Which spiritual disciplines do we need to practise? What must our personal priorities be if we want to stay faithful to God in our 'Babylon'? For some ideas, look at:
   *   2 Timothy 1:13–14 and 2:2

   *   Hebrews 10:24–25

   *   1 Peter 2:11–12

♥ LIVING IT OUT

9. How does the story of Daniel encourage you to be a faithful witness in your:
    - workplace?

    - family?

    - community?

10. Which steps do you need to take to look after your own spiritual life, so that you are able to be faithful to God in today's society?

▲ PRAYER TIME

Spend time praying – for yourself and for others (if you are doing this study in a group) – for the particular areas of life in which you feel your 'exile' most keenly. These could include, for example:

- strained relationships with non-Christian family members
- uncertainty about how to begin sharing the gospel with an unbelieving friend
- concerns about being marginalized at work for your Christian values
- seeking ways to make a God-glorifying impact on your community

Pray for God's strength to stay faithful wherever he has placed you. Rejoice because your time of exile is almost over; you are on your way home!

 FURTHER STUDY

Like Daniel, Joseph is a Bible character who interacted with foreign rulers, contributed to the prosperity of his adopted homeland and took a stand for God's values. Read his story in Genesis 37 – 50. Which principles and practices can we learn from Joseph's life about living faithfully for God in our society?

Notes for leaders

God's faithfulness to himself

1. If this is the first time your group has met, they may be hesitant to share their thoughts, so be ready to contribute ideas. Difficult circumstances, suffering and sorrow, seemingly unanswered prayers and our own disobedience all have the potential to make us question God's faithfulness. We tend to measure this faithfulness by how we perceive that God is acting towards us as individuals. The aim of this session is to help us to see that God's faithfulness is actually an inherent, immutable aspect of his character.

2. Moses asked to see God's glory; God answered by proclaiming his name and causing all his goodness, his glorious presence, to pass by. It's significant that Moses wanted to see God's glory, and God responded by talking about, and showing him, his character. God's glory is the full weight of his character, his true nature.

3. Faithfulness is part of God's character in the same way that love, grace and compassion are. It is not an add-on and can't be diminished in any way; it is who he is. His faithfulness is not meagre but 'abounding', overflowing. The faithfulness of God's character is an expression or demonstration of his glory.

4. God's faithfulness is seen in his love and forgiveness of individuals who come to him in repentance. It is also seen in his punishment of the guilty (see Exodus 20:5: his punishment is on those 'who hate me', those who refuse to repent). As a holy God, he must punish sin if he is to stay true to himself. The wonder of the gospel is that, in Jesus, God took the punishment for sin upon himself, paying its price. He was 'just and the one who justifies those who have faith in Jesus' (Romans 3:26). We are forgiven and welcomed into God's presence because God is faithful to himself in both his mercy and his justice.

5. Moses' immediate response to the revelation of God's character was to worship him. He also seemed to gain a sober appreciation of

himself and the Israelites: he repented for the people's stubbornness, pleaded again for God's presence to be with them, and asked God to take them as his 'inheritance' (that is, for the Israelites to belong to God).

6. Numbers 23:19: God's being faithful to himself means that he does not lie or change his mind. When he says he will do something, he does it. He always keeps his promises. Isaiah 55:10–11: the Word of God that once spoke the world into being has lost none of its power. The Word that God speaks, through the prophets and later the apostles, always accomplishes his purpose, whether that is to condemn, comfort, save or challenge.

7. Romans 3:3–4 teaches that God will never break his promises, even if we break ours. Paul's point is that God is keeping his promise and revealing his faithfulness to his righteous character by punishing Israel for its unbelief. 2 Timothy 2:13: our behaviour does not determine God's character. These verses are often taken out of context. The meaning is not that if I am faithless, God will remain faithful to me regardless; rather, even if I am faithless, God remains faithful to himself. He can't deny himself, his promises or purposes. This means we can be confident that we will live and reign eternally with God if we endure for him now. But if we deny him (choose to disown him), we will not spend eternity with him.

8. In Deuteronomy 32:4, Moses says God is 'the Rock'. This image conveys the truth that God is trustworthy, strong, steadfast, not easily moved, a source of refuge for those in need. He is not 'a rock' but 'the Rock': our only hope, strength and security. This picture is used throughout the Bible (2 Samuel 22:2–3; Psalm 18:2) and is often linked with salvation (Deuteronomy 32:15), underlining that our faithful God is the only way of salvation.

9. Exodus 34:8–9: our first response to God's faithfulness should be worship. As we grow in our appreciation of God's character, we recognize our own sinfulness and repent, and we understand our need for God's help and presence. Lamentations 3:19–24: God's faithfulness

in his love to us means that even in trials and sorrows, we have hope. God's love is enduring and we can experience it anew every day. We can wait on God, trusting his timing and purposes fully, because we know that he is wholly committed to us and he is faithful to his covenant promises.

10. (a) Our days are full of examples of God's faithfulness that showcase his glory. Every time God answers our prayers for strength or patience, brings the sun up or speaks to us through his Word, his glory is on display. This is a breathtaking thought. Think of specific ways in which God has shown his faithfulness this week (and in doing so, revealed his glory).

   (b) Perhaps it would help to slow down and take time to reflect each day on all the examples of God's faithfulness. Perhaps we have to alter our thinking so that, instead of focusing on all that we have achieved, we see how God's faithfulness has enabled us to complete tasks at work, serve in church or look after our family.

God's faithfulness to his promises

1. Usually, we don't feel very good about ourselves if we break a promise and let someone down. Unfortunately, sometimes our failings in this area have a lasting impact: our children lose trust in us; the boss no longer gives us significant projects to work on; or the relationship with a friend never really recovers that previous level of intimacy. Rather than focusing on the ways our broken promises hurt others, encourage the group to see how we never will experience that sort of disappointment or disillusionment with God. As a promise-keeper, he is always worthy of our trust.

2. God's promise to Abraham was to bless him and give him many descendants. Genesis 12:1–3 and 22:15–18 provide a fuller account.

3. God wanted to 'make the unchanging nature of his purpose very clear' (verse 17), that is, his purpose was still to bless his people and multiply their descendants. So, he swore by himself (because there was no higher authority to swear by). This oath was not for Abraham's benefit; he already trusted God's promise. In Genesis 22, Abraham had been prepared to sacrifice his son Isaac, trusting that God could raise his son from the dead. Amazingly, God took this oath for us. We are the ones who have 'fled to take hold of the hope set before us' (verse 18), and he wanted us to be doubly sure and 'greatly encouraged' that he would keep his promise.

4. The 'hope set before us' (verse 18) is the hope of life for ever with Christ. Hebrews 11:16 describes living for ever with Jesus as a 'better country', a 'heavenly' city. Our hope is the secure access we have to eternal life with God in his new kingdom.

5. The Bible promises that Jesus not only achieves our salvation: he anchors it in the presence of God. He has ascended into heaven, into the inner sanctuary, and he roots our salvation there, where it is safe and secure. He is the forerunner (the one that goes first), and Jesus' resurrection is the guarantee that we too will be raised to new life. Until then Jesus, our High Priest, is praying to God for us. This hope in Christ and the truths of the gospel not only gives peace to our souls but also helps us to stand firm, trusting in God's promises on difficult days.

6. God has promised that in the end times, when Christ returns, he will shake both the heavens and the earth so that only an 'unshakeable kingdom' (his kingdom shared with those who put their trust in him) remains.

7. If the Israelites had to heed God's warning from Mount Sinai, how much more do we have to heed the warning that comes from 'the city of the living God . . . the heavenly Jerusalem' (Hebrews 12:22)? We must accept the salvation that Christ won for us on the cross (verse 24) and obey God now (verse 25). Although other things can be shaken (nations, finances and health), we can trust God because we belong to a kingdom that cannot be shaken. So, our response is one of thankfulness and worship. Our worship – of lips and lives – is reverent because our God is 'a consuming fire' (verse 29). The allusion to Deuteronomy 4:24 is a reminder that God is jealous for devotion; he will judge sin. We are thankful because Jesus has paid the penalty for sin so that we can stand in the face of God's judgment.

8. Isaiah 40:29–31: we are aware of our human frailty, but God promises his help and strength to those who put their trust in him. Paul, for example, spoke about this strength in 2 Corinthians 12:9–10. Philippians 4:6–7: when we pray, with thanksgiving, presenting our requests to God, he promises an out-of-this-world peace. God will shield and protect our hearts and minds in a way that only he can. Hebrews 13:5: God promises to be with us always. There is nowhere we could go, no sin we could commit, no pit of depression so deep that it would cause us to slip out of God's loving care.

9. Sometimes we look at all that is going on in our lives and in the world, and wonder how God could be working for our good or, indeed, if he is working at all. This disconnect comes because of our limited perspective. We struggle to see how difficult situations could be for our benefit. However, God sees the full, eternal picture and he knows what our 'good', our transformation to become more like Christ, requires. We won't often see how true this promise is in real time, only with hindsight. Romans 8:28 actually offers tremendous comfort and encouragement: however dark the days, God is transforming us into the image of Christ. We shouldn't dismiss God's means of working; we shouldn't waste the suffering. Instead, we can use these times of being laid low to seek God; spend time in his Word; allow him to mould our character and priorities; learn the lessons of obedience, dependence, patience and gratitude.

10. There may be time to discuss only a few of these scenarios. The point is not to dismiss the pain and suffering many face or even to make light of it. We need to recognize and support one another as we suffer (Galatians 6:2). Jesus himself wept at the devastation that sin causes (John 11:35). But we don't grieve without hope (1 Thessalonians 4:13). Training our minds and hearts on Christ and the future glory he has promised will give us comfort and hope. We can trust God's sovereignty, knowing he promises to work all things out for our good and for his glory (Romans 8:28). Even our joys are only a shadow of what is to come, leaving us longing for more. Through all the ups and downs of life, we can cling to God's promises and, far better, we can cling to the Promise-Keeper himself.

SESSION 3

God's faithfulness to keep me

1. Difficult life circumstances, sorrows, failures, disobedience, sporadic commitment to Bible reading and prayer, and a host of other things, may make us wonder whether our faith will sustain us until the end. The aim of this study is to encourage us to press on in our devotion to God, whatever the circumstances, knowing that he promises to preserves us for our eternal inheritance.

2. God commissioned Paul to be an apostle. Notice that, throughout this passage, it is God who does the calling; it is he who takes the initiative.

3. God calls, as his people, the members of the church in Corinth, and everyone else who 'call[s] on the name of . . . Jesus Christ' (verse 2). That means those who turn to Christ for salvation, believing his death on the cross was sufficient to pay the price for sin. Because of faith in Christ and his work on the cross, we are declared 'holy' (sanctified). Note that God's call is prior to our calling: we come to Christ because God has called us.

4. (a) Jesus died on the cross, on our behalf, to pay the penalty for sin and restore us to God. It is only by calling on Jesus' name (coming to him as the only means to God) that we are saved, and his death 'sanctifies' us (declares us holy in God's sight).
   (b) In the present, Jesus continues to give us grace and equips us with spiritual gifts, so that we can live and serve him as disciples. We are united with Christ, sharing his life and a deep relationship with him.
   (c) In the future, Jesus will return.

5. God promises to be faithful. If he has called us into a relationship with Jesus, he promises to keep us persevering until Jesus returns. He will ensure that we keep on trusting in Christ, stand firm in our Christian commitment and are blameless on the last day.

6. 1 Thessalonians 5:23–24 affirms that God is faithful and can be relied on to complete the sanctifying work that he has begun in us. He is the one who will make sure that we are ready for Christ's return. Jude 1–2 asserts that being called to salvation, loved by God and kept faithful until we receive our eternal inheritance are part of one movement of God. Our salvation is entirely dependent on him: he planned it, made it possible and will bring it to completion. Here, Jesus is doing the 'keeping', underlining how Father, Son and Holy Spirit are invested in us and taking the initiative.

7. In the New Testament, baptism followed very quickly after conversion. Here, Paul is not saying that baptism saves us but that he sees baptism and conversion as one event. Baptism pictures what it means to become a Christian: we die with Christ (to our sins and old way of life), and we are raised to new life with and for him. The point is that when we become Christians, we are, in a glorious way, 'united with Christ' (connected to him); we identify with him, and all he is and does applies to us. So, if we are united with Christ in his death, then, surely, we will be united with him in resurrection.

8. God's commitment to keep us faithful to the end does not absolve us from grace-fuelled effort. Paul is emphatic in Romans 6 that our new life in Christ is not an excuse to keep on sinning; rather, it is a call to holy living. We have been sanctified by Jesus' death on the cross and now we have to learn to live as the holy people God called us to be (1 Corinthians 1). Like the Corinthians, we have been 'enriched' with spiritual gifts. God gifts us his grace, so that we can live and serve in a way which pleases him. Knowing that we will spend eternity with Jesus should shape our priorities now, encouraging us to invest our time, talents and finances in what will really last (1 Corinthians 3:10–15). See also Titus 2:11–14.

9. (a) There is no sin so big that God can't forgive it. He loves you. His faithfulness and commitment to you are dependent not on how good you have been but on the faithfulness, love and commitment of Christ. Like the father in the story of the prodigal son, God stands ready to welcome you home.

(b) We long for our children to love and follow the Lord; it is heartbreaking to watch them turn away from the faith. Urge your friend, like the persistent widow (Luke 18:1–8), to keep praying! We don't want to offer false assurance; 'hold[ing] our original conviction to the end' is key (Hebrews 3:14). But God alone knows what has gone on in the child's heart. Thank God for any interest she has shown in the past, and ask him to stir her heart again and awaken her to the truth of the gospel message.

10. God has given us the Bible, prayer, fellowship and the testimony of other believers to keep our faith 'warm', to use C. S. Lewis's analogy. Your group may come up with other ideas of how God strengthens our faith, such as through the joys of creation, technology that enables us to 'attend' church online, or serving and using our gifts. Many believers will testify that suffering has encouraged them to cling more closely to God and increase their dependence on him. Encourage individuals to look for how God is working in their lives and to cooperate with him.

God's faithfulness to forgive me

1. As I mentioned in the Introduction, we may wonder whether God runs out of patience when we commit the same sin time and again. Sometimes we may question whether our sin is too big for God to forgive. Perhaps we don't always realize the severity of sin and so don't acknowledge that it has to be forgiven. Also, the fact that Christ alone dealt with our sin is a sticking point for many. We struggle to accept God's free gift and would prefer to earn our forgiveness in some way.

2. Before David repented, he felt the full weight of his sin and guilt in his mind and body. Unconfessed sin wracked his body, sapped his strength and left him groaning (verses 3–4). By contrast, David confidently declares that the person who has received God's forgiveness is 'blessed' or happy (verses 1–2).

3. To know the blessing of verse 1, David had to uncover (expose/be honest about) his sin to God and confess it.

4. As soon as David confessed his sin, God forgave him. God's forgiveness was immediate, without qualification or fanfare.

5. Appreciating what God had done for him, David wanted others to repent and experience the same blessing, so he called people to seek God in prayer while there was still time (verse 6). Forgiven people find their refuge in God; they are teachable and obedient, trusting in his unfailing love (verses 7–10). They worship God with gladness and a full heart (verse 11).

6. From the context of 1 John 2:1, we learn that John is not referring to the forgiveness required for salvation: he is writing to believers, who still sin. The encouragement is that Christ is our advocate before God. He is interceding for us, defending our case, 'reminding' God that the

penalty for our sin has already been paid by his death on the cross. The righteousness of Christ is now our righteousness – that is our status. With the Holy Spirit's help, we strive to make our status more and more of a practical reality. John also talks about Jesus as our 'atoning sacrifice', which means that God's wrath at sin was absorbed, in Christ, at Calvary. Because Jesus took my place and suffered for my sin, I can be forgiven. His once-and-for-all death on the cross achieved forgiveness, not just for all my sin (past, present and future) but also for the sins of everyone who comes to him in repentance.

7. Psalm 103:1–4: God's forgiveness is not rationed. He forgives 'all your sins'. He doles out this benefit with 'love and compassion', which speaks of his affection. God's heart and will are invested in his forgiving us and our restoration. John 3:16: God loves us so much that he sent Jesus to die in our place, to take our punishment and bring us forgiveness. Forgiving us was so important to God that he took the initiative to orchestrate a salvation plan, one that cost him his own beloved Son. Ephesians 1:7–8: forgiveness is seen as a gift of God's grace, which he 'lavishes' on us. These verses convey the unstinting, abundant and overflowing kindness of God, who forgives and redeems us.

8. Much could be said in answer to this question. When we are forgiven, God covers our sins (verse 1). When David covered his sin, he hid it (verse 3–5), but God covers our sin in the sense that he blots it out – it is dealt with once and for all. This psalm looks forward to when Jesus' blood, shed on the cross, would cover our sin. Forgiveness also means that God does not count our sin against us. God will not remind us of our sin the next time we fail; it is not recorded for posterity. Instead, God credits us with his righteousness (verse 11; see Romans 4:7–8). Forgiveness is an act of God's grace, based on faith; it is not limited or conditional on future performance. God's forgiveness is immediate when we repent (verse 5) and restores our whole being (verses 3–4). Because God's forgiveness is readily available, he is completely trustworthy (verse 10). Now, as we seek to serve God in response to such amazing forgiveness, his 'loving eye' (verse 8) is on us and he is our 'hiding-place' (verse 7).

9. Initially, David resisted the need to repent but, eventually, he did ask God for forgiveness. As soon as he experienced the peace and joy of sins forgiven, he was passionate about encouraging others to seek forgiveness. David had a renewed passion to trust and obey God, and he worshipped God wholeheartedly. Often, we don't plead for God's forgiveness and mercy because we fail to recognize sin or realize how offensive it is. We hold tightly to sin, despite seeing its detrimental effect on ourselves (and others). It might be that we enjoy our sins and take comfort in them; perhaps we don't want to change our lifestyles; or maybe we don't want to humble ourselves before God. Of course, we can clearly see the sins of others, especially if their behaviour makes ours look good! David urges, 'Let all the faithful pray to you while you may be found' (verse 6). He encourages us to come to God for repentance while there is still time.

10. Much of the time, we will have to live with the consequences of our sins, but that is different from living with guilt. Jesus' death on the cross dealt with our sin and the feelings of guilt that accompany it (see Psalm 32:5; Isaiah 6:7; Hebrews 10:22). Satan, others and even our own conscience may remind us of past sin and resurrect our feelings of guilt. When that happens, we should go back to the cross, reflect on what Jesus has done for us and rehearse the gospel to ourselves. We can use the words of hymns (like the one below) or verses of Scripture to fill our hearts with truth. We can pray for God's peace (Philippians 4:6–7) and joy (Romans 15:13), and keep serving him wholeheartedly.

> *When Satan tempts me to despair*
> *And tells me of the guilt within,*
> *Upward I look and see him there,*
> *Who made an end to all my sin.*
> *Because the sinless Savior died,*
> *My sinful soul is counted free;*
> *For God, the just, is satisfied*
> *To look on him and pardon me.*
> (Charitie L. Bancroft, 'Before the Throne of God Above', 1863)

Our faithfulness to God in the daily routine

1. We don't want to put Christians on pedestals and idolize them. But a lot of us know older Christians who have been steadfastly devoted to God over many years, perhaps a parent, a youth group leader or an older person in our congregation. We can be encouraged and learn from their example. Their lives have often been marked by difficulty, but also by a commitment to be grateful, to serve their local community, to act with integrity and kindness in the workplace, to read the Bible and pray, to be involved in church life, to give financially to God's work and to be concerned about world mission. These are just some examples, so feel free to come up with ideas of your own.

2. Faithfulness to her mother-in-law: Ruth left her own family in Moab and accompanied her mother-in-law back to Bethlehem, a completely unknown place and people. In a foreign land, Ruth also took the initiative to find food and look after Naomi. Faithfulness in her work: Naomi and Ruth were destitute, but Ruth didn't wait for God to provide a miracle or expect her mother-in-law to tell her what to do. She got up and went to the fields to pick up leftover grain. It was an unspectacular, but necessary, first step. Once she got to the field, she worked hard and consistently. The work wasn't glamorous or without danger (verses 8–9), but she got on with it.

3. Ruth's faithfulness in her work and in the routine of life is based on the 'till death do us part' commitment she made to Naomi, her people and her God. Ruth was a foreigner, yet, staggeringly, she made a covenant commitment to the God of Israel. This new allegiance now informed every aspect of her life.

4. Boaz was so impressed that Ruth would leave her home, family and culture to be faithful to Naomi and Naomi's God that he made sure

she was safe and provided for in his fields. He was keen that God would reward her faithfulness. Little did he know that he would answer his own prayers!

5. Ruth got up and went out to work in the fields. She used her initiative, took the next step that had to be taken and she worked hard. God used her faithfulness to her mother-in-law, her dedication to hard work and her willingness to persevere in the routine of life to showcase his providential care. It so happened, under God's sovereignty, that the field Ruth chose to work in belonged to Boaz, a relative of Naomi's late husband Elimelek. Boaz promised to keep Ruth safe and provide for her. We learn later that Boaz would become Naomi and Ruth's kinsman-redeemer, the one who rescued them from poverty and made them part of his family.

6. This psalm seems to be a form of liturgy in which the congregation asks the requirements of admission into God's presence and the priest gives his reply. Instead of the answer being rituals that have to be performed, the focus is on the integrity of the worshipper, in conduct, conversation and relationships: speaking and acting honestly; keeping one's word; no unneighbourly behaviour; and no greed or corruption in financial matters. This is not a tick-list of what we have to do to enter God's presence; rather, it is a description of how people who belong to God should behave. With the Holy Spirit's help, we are to act with faithfulness in every area of our lives. (Note: 'blameless' in verse 2 isn't perfection but, instead, one whose life reflects devotion to God.)

7. 1 Peter 4:9–11: offer hospitality, using the gifts God has given us (public or behind-the-scenes gifts), not for applause or approval but in the unglamorous pursuit of serving others. These verses seem to assume regular attendance and commitment to rotas! Colossians 3:12–17: we are to reflect God's character, which means showing kindness, patience and love to one another. In church life, reflecting God's character means that we 'bear' with others, being eager to forgive, just like Christ forgave us. God, not us, is the focal point of our worship and service. 2 Corinthians 9:7: chapters 8 and 9 discuss the congregation giving a financial gift to help other poor churches.

Giving to God should come from a grateful heart and be proportionate to our means (2 Corinthians 8:12).

8. Jonathan was King Saul's son. The crown would not pass to Jonathan, however, because God had anointed David as the next king. Where we would have expected enmity, we find a deep friendship instead. Jonathan accepted God's plans for David and, instead of being jealous, was a loyal, loving friend. He was committed to David and spoke well of him to others (Saul), even when it was difficult and dangerous to do so (1 Samuel 19:4). When David was in fear of his life, Jonathan encouraged him to 'find strength in God' (1 Samuel 23:15–17). He reminded him of God's truth and purpose.

9. What would it look like to be more faithful as a parent, friend, spouse, employer, employee or church member? You won't have time to discuss what it means to be faithful in every area of life, so choose a couple of aspects and come up with some practical ideas. For example, for someone in the group, being more faithful in marriage may mean not belittling a spouse in public, even in jest. For someone else, being faithful as an employee will mean working the hours paid for, even when working from home, where no one can check.

10. The story of Ruth reminds us that, as we are faithful in the daily routine of life, God is working in his sovereignty and providential care. Even our most ordinary acts of faithfulness, such as looking after older family members or working hard to feed our families, are seen by God and can be used by him for his good purposes. Psalm 15:5: 'Whoever does these things will never be shaken.' As we trust in God to keep us faithful, he promises to hold us fast. 1 Peter 4:10: God equips us for faithfulness; he gives us gifts to use in his service. Colossians 3:12–17: God loves us, has chosen us and has made us holy in his sight (we are working out this holiness in practice). We have been forgiven by God, so we can extend forgiveness to others with the same generosity. We have the Holy Spirit, the Bible, songs and hymns, all offering help and encouragement as we persevere in our journey of faith. 2 Corinthians 9:7: our faithfulness (in this case, in financial giving) delights God's heart. 1 Samuel 23: God gives us friends to encourage us to find strength in God in difficult times.

Our faithfulness to God in hard times

1. Some in the group may want to share about deep suffering, such as bereavement, divorce or job loss. Also include in your discussions the more common, continuing struggles, such as parenting issues, looking after elderly relatives and so on. Our hardships don't necessarily bring us closer to God; we may have periods of feeling angry, confused and hurt. Acknowledge these feelings, but also encourage group members to share how dark times did bring them closer to God. For example, there might have been a fresh realization that God is our only hope and source of strength; perhaps a keener sense of his presence or an increased desire to meet with him through his Word.

2. The writer of Hebrews encourages us to fix our eyes (verse 2) – continually – on Jesus so that we don't 'grow weary and lose heart' (verse 3). Jesus is the 'pioneer and perfecter of our faith' (verse 2). He went ahead of us into God's presence and will complete our faith, so he is the perfect model for us to follow if we want to be faithful to God in hard times. We are to focus particularly on Jesus' work on the cross: he suffered and yet was faithful to God, enduring the shame and agony of Calvary, keeping his eye on the glory of being at his Father's right hand. The cross is the greatest proof of God's faithfulness to us. It is the reminder that we can trust him completely, which gives us comfort in dark days and hope for the future.

3. The 'word of encouragement' is that we are God's children; we are his sons and daughters. When we face suffering, we are tempted to think that God has forgotten us or doesn't love us. These verses indicate the exact opposite. If he didn't love and care about us like a father, he wouldn't be invested in spurring us on and bringing us to maturity. Suffering should be viewed as God's discipline, his way of chastening and rebuking us. The understanding here is that suffering is not

pointless but purposeful. God teaches, corrects and instructs us through suffering.

4. Don't make light of suffering (verse 4); don't dismiss it or treat it as unimportant. Don't lose heart either (verse 3). Keep being faithful to God through suffering; don't become discouraged or disillusioned by or disappointed in God. 'Endure hardship as a discipline' (verse 7) and persevere by recognizing suffering for what it is: not evidence of God abandoning us but proof of his fatherly love and desire for us to be like Christ. 'Submit' (verse 9), which means be willing to learn the lessons God wants to teach us; we shouldn't waste the suffering but be shaped by God through it.

5. God's discipline is for our good, so that we become more like Jesus. 'Sharing in his holiness', however, is not an automatic outcome. There are plenty of people who have become bitter rather than better because of suffering. It depends on whether we join God in his work, whether we welcome or resist the Holy Spirit's prompting. Those who are faithful through suffering, who allow themselves to be 'trained' by it, reap the rewards and share God's character. Their lives are marked more and more by God's righteousness and peace.

6. The psalmist's suffering was compounded by God's silence. God's failure to intervene in his situation and to answer his prayers caused the psalmist to question God and doubt. However, the psalmist changed his focus from himself to God. He reminded himself of God's faithfulness in the past, of his acts and miracles on behalf of the Israelites. No doubt the psalmist was thinking of the exodus. He also reminded himself of God's character, particularly his holiness. Remembering God's faithfulness in the past helped the psalmist to endure in the present, even though his own circumstances remained unchanged.

7. Knowing that our suffering is not a random accident, and that God has allowed it for a purpose, gives us the encouragement we need to press on in faith, to endure hardship with hope, and to join God in the work that he wants to achieve in and through us. 2 Corinthians

12:7b–10: Paul explains that God gave him a 'thorn in the flesh' (we don't know exactly what it was) to prevent him from becoming conceited, so that his weakness would showcase God's strength. It forced Paul to rely on God's grace rather than his own abilities. Like Paul, when we are weak, we know that God is strong. Our faithfulness in hard times is an opportunity for people to see God's grace and glory. James 1:2–4: James is honest about the fact that we *will* face 'trials of many kinds' – suffering is inevitable. He argues that we can face these difficulties with joy, not because they are easy to endure but because we know that they have a purpose. God can use our difficulties to help us to persevere in the faith, making us more mature believers. Without hardship, there would be nothing to test our faith. Each time we remain faithful through a trial, we will be more confident, in God's strength, to face the next one. As we prove God's faithfulness, we are encouraged to stay faithful.

8. Isaiah 43:1–2: God does not promise to remove the difficulties; he promises to be present with us in them. Whatever we are going through, we can be sure that God is with us, he loves us, we are his and he is in control. His presence will sustain us until the end. In 2 Corinthians 4:16–17, Paul reminds us of God's promise that he is transforming us into the likeness of Christ, and that our current troubles are temporary and insignificant compared to the glory that awaits. Of course, our suffering does not seem 'light and momentary' as we endure it, and we do not wish to minimize the pain that people might be dealing with. However, when we fix our eyes on Jesus, on what he is achieving for us and on the glory that will be revealed, this gives us an eternal perspective and helps us to persevere.

9. (a) Like the psalmist, remembering God's faithfulness in the past does encourage us to press on in faithfulness. It reminds us that God is at work, that he is *for* us, that prayer works, that God knows the big picture and will work all things out in his time and for his good purpose.

   (b) Reflecting on God's dealings with us in the past may also remind us of a time when we were closer to God, when we were more prayerful, more dedicated to meeting God in his Word, and more committed to our church family and Christian service. In God's strength, use these promptings to pursue and return to a deeper relationship with him.

10. If possible, encourage the group to be specific in their responses. However, sometimes we just don't know what God is achieving through our suffering. If that is the case, we can still be confident that he wants to use these difficult days to draw us closer to himself, to 'share in his holiness' (Hebrews 12:10). If we are not going through difficult times now, let's ask God to help us to remember these truths in the future.

Our faithfulness to God as citizens in society

1. God is at work in many ways in our generation. For example, the increased online presence of churches and Christian organizations is bringing the gospel straight into people's homes. Many people, precisely because they have not been brought up knowing about Christianity, are curious and very open to hearing about Jesus. The aim of this study is not to be overly pessimistic about the state of Christianity but to point out that the goal posts have shifted. We need to rethink how we share our faith and live faithfully.

2. Nebuchadnezzar, the Babylonian king, besieged Jerusalem, ransacked the temple, carried off the king, and took some of the brightest and best young men to serve in his palace. Daniel and his friends were taken away from the home, culture, people and language that they knew. In contrast to their dreams and expectations, they began three years of rigorous training in the language and literature of Babylon. The shock, dislocation and newness of all Daniel experienced can't be underestimated.

3. Daniel seemed to accept readily his new training regime and the expectation that he would serve in the king's palace. He also accepted his new name. However, Daniel 'resolved' (was determined) not to eat the food and wine from the king's table. He didn't want to 'defile' himself; perhaps he considered this food unclean according to the Old Testament laws; perhaps the food had been offered to idols; or perhaps Daniel considered this an area in which it was possible for him to resist the assimilation process (he didn't have much choice about his education plan or his new name). Whatever the reasons, he stood by his convictions.

4. Daniel is portrayed as honourable, gracious and wise in the manner of his opposition. He *'asked ... for permission not to defile himself'* (verse 8) instead of simply objecting. Rather than outright rebellion, he came up with a workable solution. He proposed a ten-day diet of water and vegetables, and then an assessment of how healthy he and his friends were (verses 12–13). Daniel's attitude was such that he won over the guard. His faithfulness to God was winsome and attractive.

5. God did not abandon the exiles in Babylon; he was still sovereign. He caused the official to show favour to Daniel concerning his new diet. God also gave the young Israelite men in the king's court gifts to understand Babylonian literature. Daniel, in particular, was given the gift of interpreting dreams and visions. Having these gifts didn't mean that Daniel and his friends did not apply themselves to their learning, but simply that God prospered them. They outstripped their contemporaries in learning and understanding, and their excellence even caught the eye of the king.

6. (a) Despite being in exile and forced to work for a foreign king, Daniel excelled. He was promoted to become one of the top three rulers who directly reported to King Darius. His work was so exceptional that the king was going to put him in charge of the whole kingdom. His opponents could find no fault with his work ethic and integrity: there was no corruption, no negligence; he was completely trustworthy. If they wanted to topple him, they would have to resort to challenging his faith. They knew that Daniel would be faithful to God, so they encouraged the king to issue an irrevocable edict forbidding prayer to anyone other than him, which would inevitably trap Daniel.

   (b) Prayer three times a day was a habit that Daniel had cultivated. When this crisis came, it did not *make* Daniel a man of prayer; it exposed him as one. This spiritual discipline was deeply ingrained in Daniel, sustained his faith in exile and revealed his dependence on God.

   (c) Daniel was not deterred by this ban on praying, indicating that he was wholeheartedly committed to worshipping God and honouring the first commandment. He wouldn't worship any other idols (that is, the king), even if it meant compromising his own safety or, indeed, his own life. He wouldn't deny, demean or entertain anything that would compromise his faith in God, even to honour the king.

7. The Israelites were not just to endure being exiles, they were to settle well in the land, building homes and raising families. More than that, they were to pray and do all that they could do to prosper Babylon. Often, we are tempted to retreat into a Christian bubble, ignore all that is going on in the world and simply have Bible studies while we wait for Jesus to return to make all things new. Jeremiah's charge to the exiles indicates that we have to engage with our world; we are to pray and seek its prosperity. We must live for God here and now. Our present circumstances are not merely to be endured; they are an opportunity to live out God's kingdom values and bring his peace to the world.

8. 2 Timothy 1:13–14 and 2:2: these charges of Paul were initially to Timothy and then to church leaders, but they have implications for us all. With the Holy Spirit's help, we have to 'guard' the gospel, which would seem to indicate protecting its content (not adding to it or taking anything away); making sure it is communicated often and well (in various contexts, such as preaching, small groups, to our children, and so on); treasuring it in our own lives; and not letting false teachers corrupt it. 2 Timothy 2:2 particularly emphasizes the need to hand this truth down to the next generation by passing it on to reliable people who can teach others. Investing in the teaching and training of the next generation of believers is crucial. Hebrews 10:24–25: don't give up meeting with other believers. We need others to spur us on in the faith, to point us to Jesus, to keep us accountable, to experience the joy of serving and worshipping together, and to help to carry our burdens. 1 Peter 2:11–12: we have to strive for holiness, and never give up the grace-fuelled effort of saying 'no' to sin and 'yes' to godliness (Titus 2:11–14). It is easy for exiles to adapt to the culture of their surroundings, but we must live as citizens of God's kingdom,

displaying his values and priorities. Our lifestyle and good deeds should be such that, even if people don't like them, they can't help but glorify God because of them, either when God judges them or when they come to salvation.

9. Encourage the group to think of how to apply the different elements of Daniel's story to their own contexts. For example, what do we learn about being a winsome witness, about integrity at work, about standing up for godly principles graciously and wisely, about the need to develop holy habits and about honouring God rather than people?

10. Think about your answers to question 8 and what you have learnt from the life of Daniel. Be specific about which steps (with the Holy Spirit's help) you have to take to strengthen your faith. For example, spending more time in prayer and Bible reading, memorizing Scripture, renewing your commitment to the church and Christian service, reading good Christian books and biographies, tackling a particular sin or making an effort to deepen your fellowship with other believers.

Publications mentioned in the text

Books

Joel Beeke, *Knowing and Growing in Assurance of Faith* (Christian Focus, 2017)

Jerry Bridges, *The Gospel for Real Life: Turn to the Liberating Power of the Cross Every Day* (NavPress, 2002)

Jerry Bridges, *Transforming Grace* (NavPress, 2017)

D. A. Carson, *How Long, O Lord? Reflections on Suffering and Evil* (IVP, 1990)

Kevin DeYoung, *What Does the Bible Really Teach about Homosexuality?* (IVP, 2015)

Greg Gilbert, *Assured: Discover Grace, Let Go of Guilt, and Rest in Your Salvation* (Baker, 2019)

Sharon Hastings, *Wrestling with My Thoughts: A Doctor with Severe Mental Illness Discovers Strength* (IVP, 2020)

Timothy Keller, *Walking with God through Pain and Suffering* (Hodder & Stoughton, 2013)

Michael Kelley, *Boring: Finding an Extraordinary God in an Ordinary Life* (Broadman & Holman, 2013)

C. S. Lewis, *Mere Christianity* (HarperCollins, 2001)

C. S. Lewis, *The Voyage of the Dawn Treader* (HarperCollins, 2009)

Rebecca McLaughlin, *Confronting Christianity: 12 Hard Questions for the World's Largest Religion* (Crossway, 2019)

Paul Mallard, *Invest Your Suffering: Unexpected Intimacy with a Loving God* (IVP, 2013)

Paul Mallard, *Staying Fresh: Serving with Joy* (IVP, 2015)

Glenna Marshall, *Everyday Faithfulness: The Beauty of Ordinary Perseverance in a Demanding World* (Crossway, 2020)

Glen Scrivener, *321: The Story of God, the World and You* (10Publishing, 2014)

Paul David Tripp, *Suffering: Gospel Hope When Life Doesn't Make Sense* (Crossway, 2018)
Kristen Wetherall and Sarah Walton, *Hope When It Hurts: Biblical Reflections to Help You Grasp God's Purpose in Your Suffering* (The Good Book Company, 2017)

Online publications
Ray Ortlund, 'In Between', The Gospel Coalition, 25 February 2013, <www.thegospelcoalition.org/blogs/ray-ortlund/in-between>, accessed 12 January 2021.
Paul Tripp, 'Each Morning in Ministry', The Gospel Coalition, 9 September 2012, <www.thegospelcoalition.org/article/each-morning-in-ministry>, accessed 12 January 2021.

About Keswick Ministries

Our purpose

Keswick Ministries exists to inspire and equip Christians to love and live for Christ in his world.

God's purpose is to bring his blessing to all the nations of the world (Genesis 12:3). That promise of blessing, which touches every aspect of human life, is ultimately fulfilled through the life, death, resurrection, ascension and future return of Christ. All the people of God are called to participate in his missionary purposes, wherever he may place them. The central vision of Keswick Ministries is to see the people of God equipped, inspired and refreshed to fulfil that calling, directed and guided by God's Word in the power of his Spirit, for the glory of his Son.

Our priorities

There are three fundamental priorities which shape all that we do as we look to serve the local church.

- *Hearing God's Word*: the Scriptures are the foundation for the church's life, growth and mission, and Keswick Ministries is committed to preach and teach God's Word in a way that is faithful to Scripture and relevant to Christians of all ages and backgrounds.

- *Becoming like God's Son*: from its earliest days, the Keswick movement has encouraged Christians to live godly lives in the power of the Spirit, to grow in Christlikeness and to live under Christ's lordship in every area of life. This is God's will for his people in every culture and generation.

- *Serving God's mission*: the authentic response to God's Word is obedience to his mission, and the inevitable result of Christlikeness is sacrificial service. Keswick Ministries seeks to encourage committed discipleship in family life, work and society, and energetic engagement in the cause of world mission.

Our ministry

- *Keswick Convention*. The Convention attracts some 12,000 to 15,000 Christians from the UK and around the world to Keswick every summer. It provides Bible teaching for all ages, vibrant worship, a sense of unity across generations and denominations, and an inspirational call to serve Christ in the world. It caters for children of all ages and offers a strong youth and young adult programme. And it all takes place in the beautiful Lake District – a perfect setting for rest, recreation and refreshment.

- *Keswick fellowship*. For more than 140 years, the work of Keswick has affected churches worldwide, not just through individuals being changed but also through Bible conventions that originate or draw their inspiration from the Keswick Convention. Today, there is a network of events that share Keswick Ministries' priorities across the UK and in many parts of Europe, Asia, North America, Australia, Africa and the Caribbean. Keswick Ministries is committed to strengthening the network in the UK and beyond through prayer, news and cooperative activity.

- *Keswick teaching and training*. Keswick Ministries is developing a range of inspiring, Bible-centred teaching and training that focuses on equipping believers for 'whole-of-life' discipleship. This builds on the same concern that started the Convention, that all Christians live godly lives in the power of the Spirit in all spheres of life in God's world. Some of the smaller and more intensive events focus on equipping attendees, while others focus on inspiring them. Some are for pastors, others for those in different forms of church leadership, while many are for any Christian. The aim of all the courses is for participants to return home refreshed to serve.

- *Keswick resources*. Keswick Ministries produces a range of books, devotionals, study guides and digital resources to inspire and equip the church to live for Christ. The printed resources focus on the core foundations of Christian life and mission, and help the people of God in their walk with Christ. The digital resources make teaching and sung worship from the Keswick Convention available in a variety of ways.

Our unity

The Keswick movement worldwide has adopted a key Pauline statement
to describe its gospel inclusivity: 'All one in Christ Jesus' (Galatians 3:28).
Keswick Ministries works with evangelicals from a wide variety of church
backgrounds, on the understanding that they share a commitment to the
essential truths of the Christian faith as set out in our statement of belief.

Our contact details

T: 017687 80075
E: info@keswickministries.org
W: www.keswickministries.org
Mail: Keswick Ministries, Rawnsley Centre, Main Street, Keswick,
Cumbria CA12 5NP, England

Related titles from IVP

KESWICK FOUNDATIONS

Sent
Serving God's Mission
Tim Chester

ISBN: 978 1 78359 654 6
£4.99, 80 pages, paperback

Mission is for everyone. Ordinary people can step out to become part of the most exciting, amazing, continuing adventure in the history of the world. Mission begins on our doorstep, but it reaches far beyond. It involves praying, giving and going.

Sent: Serving God's Mission offers a job description. We go right back to the character of God and see how the concept of mission unfolds throughout the storyline of the Bible.

Praise:

'Tim is one of the world's clearest and most compelling mission teachers . . . [here is] a treasure trove for us to take back to our families and home groups.' **Anna Bishop**

'I love the way this study guide so clearly teaches us the Bible, to encourage us to reach out to the world in evangelism.' **Rico Tice**

Available from your local Christian bookshop or **www.ivpbooks.com**

Related titles from IVP

KESWICK STUDY GUIDE

Longing
Elizabeth McQuoid

ISBN: 978 1 78359 934 9
£5.99, 80 pages, paperback

We are made for intimacy and purpose. We long to be happy and whole, and to be thrilled and fascinated. God created us this way; it's how we are wired. Work, money, friendship, sex, art, holidays . . . offer a temporary fix, but leave us craving for something more: more permanent, more meaningful, more beautiful. Just more.

Longing is awoken in us when we experience the brokenness of a fallen world, when there's an intangible void to fill or a higher level of beauty to attain.

This six-session study guide invites us to turn to God to satisfy our deepest longings. We may not fully realize it but, ultimately, our longing is for him.

Praise:

'A Christian is not one who has stopped all sinning, but one who has begun to feel a new longing – for the Saviour. A heart that desires Jesus is alive and growing.' **Ray Ortlund**

'Rich in biblical truth, as well as practical application . . . Short but powerful, this book will minister to both your head and heart.' **Emma Scrivener**

Related titles from IVP

Radical Gratitude
Recalibrating Your Heart in an Age of Entitlement
Peter Maiden

ISBN: 978 1 78974 185 8
£9.99, 160 pages, paperback

As Christians, we should be the most grateful people alive. After all, doesn't the Bible encourage thankfulness and condemn grumbling?

Peter Maiden traces the theme of thanksgiving in Scripture. He shows how we can genuinely live counter-cultural lives – even in an age of rampant entitlement. With a pastoral heart, he explains how gratitude is the key to joyful, consistent Christian living, discipleship and mission involvement.

Praise:

'A profoundly biblical alternative – a gospel duty and privilege, and a mark of faith.' **D. A. Carson**

'A hugely refreshing, encouraging and life-changing read.' **Jonathan Lamb**

'Inspiring and moving.' **Paul Mallard**

'Wisdom, experience and biblical insight flow through every page.' **Rebecca Manley Pippert**

'Intimate and challenging.' **Lawrence Tong**